HIS TURN
When Enough Was Enough

By
Joe McClure
Arthur Washington
Jefferson Jones
Dominic D. Davis
Kanshasa T. Downs

H.I.S.

**Forward and Introduction written by
Dr. Karen D. Lomax**

Published by:
H.I.S.
KAIROS Literary Agency
Oceanside, CA
kairosagent72@gmail.com

Editor: Dr. Karen D. Lomax
Cover design: Dr. Karen D. Lomax
Cover photo: Dr. Karen D. Lomax

Scripture quotations are KJV unless otherwise marked.

Forward

In 2012, God placed on my heart a ministry geared towards men. I had no idea where to begin or even how to get it started. Me? An outreach for men? Did God forget that I was a woman? No. He knew exactly what He was doing and why! Later, I discovered that it was a prelude to my purpose. So, in 2017, four of my fellow brothers in-Christ and I launched H.I.S. *(Healing, Inspiring, Supporting) Men's Outreach Ministry.* So, it's no surprise when the opportunity came for other members of the ministry to share their stories with the world, I accepted the invitation to write the forward with a humble spirit and gratitude in my heart. I have written my fair share of books and participated in countless writing projects, but never have I been moved as spiritually and emotionally as I have been with this next bestseller, *His Turn: When Enough Was Enough.* These five writers left no stone unturned as they unashamedly share their anger, pain, disappointment, joy, and contentment. This anthology is a reminder that it's ok to reach out and ask for help. They express how no one is exempt from the tests and trials of life, and this book is a testament that an encounter with God can change your mind and your life. I could go on and on, but these are their testimonies to share and stories to tell. It is my prayer that you don't just read their words, but feel their hearts.

Dr. Karen D. Lomax, L.H.D., MA-HSC-LF, M.Div.

Dr. Karen D. Lomax

President & Founder,
H.I.S. Men's Outreach Ministry
Karen Lomax Ministries
H.E.R.R.S. LLC
KAIROS Literary Agency

Email: chaplomax72@gmail.com
Website: karenlomaxministries.org

Table of Contents

H.I.S.

Healing, Inspiring, Supporting

Introduction

Everyone experiences up and downs in their lives, but there comes a time when you have to tell yourself, "enough is enough" and do whatever is necessary to make changes. *HIS Turn: When Enough was Enough* is an anthology based on the lives and experiences of five men of God who soon find out what they thought they had control over, actually had control over them. They share how they came face-to-face with death, abuse, addictions, and infidelity. They soon discovered the sting of the inevitable fall that comes when we seek to do things our way. The reader is taken on an emotional roller coaster as these authors share their stories of tests, trials, and triumphs with honestly and transparency. Further, the reader will see how the same God that delivered Daniel out of the lion's den, is the same God that can pull anyone out of whatever situation they get themselves into.

HIS Turn: When Enough was Enough is a must read and an excellent addition to every leader's library. It is my sincere prayer that the following testimonies will make you to rethink where you are in your life and have a real encounter with God. You do not have to live defeated! Enough is enough!

Dr. Karen D. Lomax

Why I Decided to Give My Life to God
Joe D. McClure

I had lived life the way I wanted, and that meant any way I wanted to live it. In the streets, I had so many names, but the main one was "Crazy Joe." When people would say, "Here comes Crazy Joe!" I would give them what they were looking... a show. I had to act the part and drugs and alcohol made it easy. After all, when you drink too much, you really do act crazy. My so-called friends got a kick out of seeing me act a fool and at the time, I didn't care what they were saying about me. I never took the time to think about right or wrong because I was too busy doing whatever and whenever.

Now I have always known that there as a God, but I figured if He didn't bother me, I wasn't going to say anything to Him. In my way of thinking, whatever was going to happen to me was just going to happen anyways. That's the way I had always been, so what need was there for me to change now? Hanging in the streets was far more fun and exciting than being at home, watching television and being angry with myself and those around me. You see, it's hard trying to be right all of the time and thinking everyone else is wrong because you say so. Not to mention, the people you hang with the most are the ones that will side with you regardless…right or wrong. After all, you're buddies and buddies stick with each other no matter what.

People would often ask, "Why does he act like that? Or live that? Why is he out there like that?" Those on the outside can see things in you that you can't see or you're not looking for. In the back of my mind, I knew that I was living a destructive lifestyle, but it was exciting at the time. So, I just continued down this same old road, doing the same old thing, not thinking about tomorrow or the consequences of my actions. Oftentimes, we can't see the quicksand until we have stepped into it and we are waist-deep, looking for help. When we get in trouble, it seems like no one is around and no help is available on our right or our left. All of a sudden, those who were so intrigued with you acting fool, has something better to do than to help you. I was out here all alone and everything started to catch up with me. There was nothing left for me to do, except to do what we all do when we get in over our heads, call on Jesus!

I went and talked to a preacher to seek advice and he told me to come to church and let him pray for me. I told him the church was full of those hypocrites and he told me that one more won't hurt. Reluctantly, I went. What did I have to lose? Going to church didn't help me with my problem, but it gave me some comfort to know I had someone to talk to. Further, I had more time to reflect on my life while I as locked away in a treatment program for 180 days. That's when I began to read my Bible and learned how to pray. I didn't just pray for myself, but for others who came to me for prayer.

When we get in trouble, we make all kinds of promises to God, if He would help this time, and what we would do in return. God, being who He is, worked it out for me and put me back in a good place. He cleaned up my mess and blessed me. But, old habits are hard to break. Old friends are hard to leave behind. Old places are hard to stay away from. I told myself that I wasn't going to do the same things that got me into trouble. But, that didn't last long. My job was a night job, so that kept me out of the streets. This job did random drug tests, so that kept me off drugs. I was a forklift operator, and one night, my lift ran over my foot. I immediately called on God and He came to my rescue. I was taken to the hospital in St. Louis, where I had to have two of my toes surgically removed from my left foot. NOW, God had my full attention! I was grounded for a few months and I had to learn how to walk all over again. As soon as I was healed and my foot got better, you guessed it, right back to being my old self again. I wasn't ready to commit to God. All of those things, that I told God I was going to do, had gone right out of the window.

You know God never forgets, but He forgives. When I thought I was getting away with something, He let me know, "Not this time!" One day a friend was visiting and all day long, he and I sat on my porch, smoking and drinking. I hadn't eaten anything because I was too busy having a good time. But this would turn out to be the day that would be the ending of all of the mess that I had been doing. Normally, my wife would work late, but this day she didn't. She was doing laundry and I started to sweat and feel weak. I went inside the house and lay on the floor. I called out to her for help because I could not move. My blood sugar had dropped and my blood pressure was dangerously low. She gave me some juice and started fanning me. That was enough for me! I made up my mind that if I came through this episode, I was going to do ALL the things God wanted me to do.

One day, my sister-in-law called me and said that I should read Psalms 51:10 and to read it over and over every day. So, all day, I would walk around saying, "Create in me a clean heart, O God; and renew a right spirit within me." I started telling God I was sorry for all of the wrong that I had done, and I mean EVERYTHING, and asked for forgiveness. I began to thank Him for all He had done for me and thanked Him for my new life. Most of all, I thanked Him for my wife, who stuck with me through all of my mess! If she wasn't there with me that day, I may not be here, today, telling my story. Romans 8:28 says, "And we know that all things work together for good to them that love God, to them who are the called according to his purpose."

That was enough! I had made up my mind to let God take control of my life because I had not done a good job running it myself. I love the Lord, and now I know I have been called, I have been chosen, and I know my purpose, "Study to shew thyself approved unto God, a workman that needeth not to be ashamed, rightly dividing the word of truth." God wants me to know the word, so I can spread the word, and tell the truth, "Jesus saith unto him, I am the way, the truth, and the life: no man cometh unto the Father, but by me." I can't say anything about anyone else, but as for me and my house, we will serve the Lord! I pray my testimony has encouraged you and inspired

you to draw closer to God.

Dedicated to my wife, Martha, my girls; Karen and Shanell, and to all those who may be struggling with peer pressure, alcohol and drug addiction.

Joe D. McClure

Joe D. McClure was born and raised in Southeast Missouri and is one of nine children of the late Joe McClure, Sr. and Emma Jane McClure. Joe is a veteran of the United States Marine Corps and proud husband of Martha McClure, and the father of two girls; Dr. Karen D. Lomax of Oceanside, California and Shanell Dawn McClure of Clarksville, Tennessee. Joe loves the Lord and has served in ministry for 10 years. He began his ministry under the leadership of

Bishop Johnny Roy Williams in Poplar Bluff Missouri

and is currently serving under the leadership of Pastor

Normal Cole, Jr at "Household of Faith Outreach

Ministry" in Sikeston, Missouri.

Support Joe D. McClure

Email: mcclurejoe08@gmail.com

Facebook: www.facebook.com/joe.mcclure.969

Psalm 121

¹ I will lift up mine eyes unto the hills, from whence cometh my help.

² My help cometh from the LORD, which made heaven and earth.

³ He will not suffer thy foot to be moved: he that keepeth thee will not slumber.

⁴ Behold, he that keepeth Israel shall neither slumber nor sleep.

⁵ The LORD is thy keeper: the LORD is thy shade upon thy right hand.

⁶ The sun shall not smite thee by day, nor the moon by night.

⁷ The LORD shall preserve thee from all evil: he shall preserve thy soul.

⁸ The LORD shall preserve thy going out and thy coming in from this time forth, and even for evermore.

When It Was Enough
Arthur D. Washington, Sr.

My enough began when I was deployed to Iraq on March 3, 2003. During one of those hot days in Iraq, we were at a worship service and the preacher of the hour had spoken these powerful words to me, "You have less than 48 hours to contact your wife and when you speak to her, you need to let her begin to heal." The only issue about being in Iraq was trying to get phone service to call back to Germany. Sometimes it was a hit and miss. The week prior to me receiving the message, I was unable to reach my family. By the grace of God, I was able to reach my wife on the same day, but what unfolded before me was God working His plan and getting my attention. The first move of God, before this critical Sunday, occurred when God took me from my family and placed me in a place of Isolation where I could only see and hear from Him.

Secondly, I had withheld a secret from my wife that could have cost me my marriage. In my phone conversation with my wife, I shared that I was a victim of sexual assault from the age of nine until the age of eleven. The phone went silent, and when you hear dead silence, you might as well say, "HOUSTON WE HAVE A PROBLEM." I was not sure that after my deployment, if I was going to still have a wife. For 10 years, I had withheld this from my wife and now sharing this was not good. One thing I have realized is that God has a way of getting things clear and out in the open.

The third and final situation really shook the core of my foundation. There is a saying, "Strange things occur at midnight." This was not strange, for me, but God knew what He was doing and had it set

16

up that way. As you recall, I mentioned that I had received the message from the Preacher, "You got 48 hours to reach your wife." Well, it was midnight and as I entered the tent area where that I shared with four other Battle Buddies, no one was there but me. This was strange at the time, but nothing that God does is out of order. At this point, God is really weighing heavy on my mind. I start to read a book entitled "The Power of a Praying Husband" by Stormie Omartian. In her book, she is telling how she grew up and the mental abuse she went through, trying to find a church that has Christian counseling as a part of the ministry. By this time, what I am reading is getting my attention, but after reading the next couple of pages, I felt I was reading about myself.

In this section of reading, Mrs. Omartian has found the counselor and is now meeting with the individual. During this particular session, the counselor states, "I want you to go home and write down every sin you have ever committed and bring it in to our next session, and I will have another counselor here in that session." The next session occurs and she brings in stacks of papers of all the sins she has ever committed. As the other counselor comes in, she is asked to place her hand on top of the pile while both counselors place their hands on hers and they pray. They say, "You are forgiven now you can get rid of the papers." At this point, a light has hit my mind. If she was able to do this, I know I need to as well. Unlike Stormie, I had stepped outside of my marriage and God had to get me to a place where it was just He and I.

After reading that portion of the book, I went looking for scraps of paper and I began writing down every sin I could remember. After about an hour, I had all these loose pieces of papers and I went outside. It is about 2 am or so, and I took my cigarette lighter with me. The air as cool with a slight breeze and I looked around to ensure I was by myself. I lifted those papers to God and I say "Lord, I ask for forgiveness of all the sins I have committed and I promise, Lord, that I will confess to my wife what I had done and I will correct that wrong in Jesus name. Then, I burned the papers (sins) and the only person who knew was God and I. But how many of us know that when you make a promise to God that you have to follow through? Well let's just say I became extremely hard headed and I could hear my mom say, "A hard head will make a soft behind".

Let's fast forward. I redeployed from Iraq, things are good, and I am waiting for my family to arrive back to Germany. It is now August and my family arrives back from the states and it is my daughter's birthday. As I am loading my family in the vehicle, I hear God say to me, "Are you going to tell your wife?" I say to myself, "Right now? No way!" So I quench my spirit and shrug it off. Yet, again, how many of us know that when you make a promise to God He is going to test you to see if you're to keep your word? Out of the blue, my wife asked me, "Did you cheat on me while you were deployed?" My response was, "No, I did not cheat on you while on my deployment." I thought I was in the clear, but God did not forget my promise I made to Him.

Over the next several days, I started to get sick, and I never really get sick. I may catch a slight cold, but nothing like this! I woke up with an upset stomach and couldn't eat, but I made it through the day. We went and saw friends and I thought this stomach bug would be over in a couple days. However, it turned out to be a nightmare! I started getting weak, my vision became blurry, and I had no strength to drive. I almost got into an accident while driving my son. It was becoming harder to get up two flights of stairs without losing my breath. Finally I went to go see the German doctor, who said I had a high temperature of 104.2. You could have cooked an egg on my back and my body was aching. With each passing day, I was getting worse. In three days, I went from being able to eat to only being able to drink.

I had all I could take! I went next door to the Army Clinic and slowly made my way to be seen. I mentioned I was on quarters and my situation was not getting better. My unit and the clinic made arraignments for me to be taken to the Army hospital in Heidelberg, Germany. While enroute, I am trying to contact my battle buddy and prayer partner, Lamonte, who works at the hospital, but I could not reach him. We get to the hospital, and I walk in looking grey and feeling like Lazarus. The staff begins to ask me questions and my response is not good. My wife happens to bump into Lamonte. He was off that day, but he had to bring his son in for an appointment. She tells him what is going on and he comes to see me. While we talk, unbeknownst to me, I have blood clots and I'm sitting on death's door step. Lamonte was informed on what was going with me, but he did not share what he knew with me. Later, I found out that he called his wife and told her to call the prayer warriors and start praying now!

The events, that occurred the next morning, are still fresh in my mind. I had heard and read of stories of people having encounters with God. I am a believer and can understand. I woke up that morning and my bed was extremely wet due to my fever going down. It only occurred in the mornings, but this particular morning, would not be the same. I tried to get out of bed, but something was wrong. I could only move my head from left to right. I looked away from the window, toward the door, and then straight to the ceiling. Then, I hear a soft voice that says" Are you going to tell her? Are you going to tell her?" Finally, I say, "Yes, Lord, I will tell her." We know God knows everything about us because He created us. God did not trust me and He knew my every move. So, as I am telling God "Yes," guess who walks through the door? Yep, my wife!

The next five minutes were the longest in my life! "Hi, honey, I have something to tell you. I cheated on you and had an affair." I saw my life flash before my eyes. My wife told me, "As soon as you heal, I am going to kick your ass!" At this point, I thought it couldn't get any worse. I was told there was nothing else that the Army hospital could do for me and I was being transferred to the German hospital. It wasn't so much as being transferred, but the looks I got from the nurses and the staff. They looked as though I was dead already. My wife looked as though she was ready to take me out of this world and who could blame her? Lamonte was praying and trying to encourage my wife, but she was not having it nor hearing it!

That was the first time I really felt like I was by myself. Even though I felt alone, God was with me. He sent His angels from my church and prayer warriors from the states were sending up prayers for me, including my fathers in the ministry. God had to show me who was in charge and to be careful what you promise God you are going to do, then go back on your word. That moment, and experience changed my life forever. God could have taken my life, but I am still here to share my story. I believe there is a greater purpose on my life and I am thankful for another chance to fulfill it. Please hear my story and allow my testimony to encourage you and give you hope.

Dedicated to my rib, Salintha, and my children; AD II and Andrea. I thank God for your encouragement and never giving up on me. Lord, thank You for allowing this servant to give unselfishly.

Arthur D. Washington, Sr.

Arthur D. Washington Sr. is a native of Gary, Indiana. He and his wife, Salintha, have been married for 23 years and have two children; Andrea age 22 and Arthur II, age 20. Arthur has served in the United States Army for 21 years and is currently stationed at Ft. Hood, Texas. Arthur has been in ministry for 24 years with the A.M.E. Church and currently serves on the staff at Anderson Chapel African Methodist Episcopal Church in Killeen, Texas. In addition, Arthur sits on the Executive Board of "Teach Them To Love

(T3L) Outreach Ministries" in Killeen, Texas and is a proud member of Phi Beta Sigma Fraternity, Inc.

Support Arthur D. Washington, Sr.

Email: arthur.washington92@gmail.com

Facebook: https://www.facebook.com/art.washington

Instagram: @art.washington_1914

Passivity, Procrastination, and No More Passes

Jefferson J. Jones

"I wish life had a rewind app. I need a scene edit for my past." by _____. Could your name go in that space? I know my name can go there. However, Romans 8:28 reminds me that I "Know that in all things God works for the good of those who love him, who have been called according to his purpose." As I reflect over my story and the layers that exist, I see how some parts bring me to the place of sharing my broken places to bring healing to yours. It's been a 30 plus year journey of dealing with that part of me that wants to just let things ride, wait until later, and/or give people another chance. Now, take a deep breath and remember this as you read: **Passivity is in the foundation of the unaccomplished.**

As a man, what is that "thing" that causes your eyes to sweat a little bit? Or maybe your seasonal allergies act up when you think about that event that you could have handled differently. Most people call "eye sweating" or "seasonal allergies" something that men typically don't like to mention. They're called tears: the tears that flow because of an emotional response to pain, hurt, regret, happiness, excitement, self-disappointment, etc. In this case, these tears are connected to that feeling of regret or even wishing that you could have responded differently. The what-if's, should-have's, and could-have's begin to roll through your mind.

Let's go back to 1994 when I was 14 years old. I was young, passive, kind, nerdy, and athletic. I realize now that when you're a kid, the other word for passive is "wimp". Okay—I'll say it. I was a little bit of a wimp. I was in the marching band, played basketball, and a gifted student. I was a marching, athletic, nerdy, and semi-cool wimp. I didn't really know how to stand up for myself when I needed to do so.

What I'm about to tell you sounds like the story of David and Goliath. Just subtract all of the weapons, fighting for the Lord, and shrink Goliath to about 5 feet and 4 inches. Maybe this is nothing like David and Goliath after all. It was a hot summer day after school in the lag time between school dismissal and band practice. I was 6 feet and 2 inches tall and every bit of 165 pounds of pure skin and bone. This mini-Goliath was a muscle head and a nice guy until I said his last name wrong. We were standing outside of the gym where there was nothing but concrete. There was a small audience to watch this battle go down. I said his name wrong on purpose, not realizing that he would go to the extreme. And then what seemed like the end of the world happened. He came at me and picked me up and slammed me on the ground. I guess the only part of this that was a battle was my body hitting the ground. I know you want to know what happened next and it will come out a little later. Even in this moment I didn't try to fight back and didn't even try to run. I chose to be passive in that moment. Maybe you can think of a time in your life in the past or even now that you wish you would have done something in that moment. What are you doing to go from passive to proactive in your life? What's stopping you from being proactive instead of passive?

As a teenager, there are other stories that I could share to show the passive nature that I displayed in my life. This passivity wasn't isolated to one event but evident in other areas of my life. As a teen, I didn't have people in my life that could speak to this area of my life. People could see my behaviors and only address my actions with no solution to deal with the root. **Until you are willing to go beneath the surface, you will continue to bear fruit that reflect your root system.** Until you deal with the underlying issues of why you avoid conflict or run when things get hard, you will continue the pattern of passivity.

This passivity that was deeply embedded in my root system began to show up in my work ethic in school and what would seem to be the simple task of getting things done. I've mentioned that I was a nerdy kid that did well in school. Once I got to undergrad, I realized that intelligence wasn't enough. At this new level, it would take intelligence, discipline, and a proactive attitude in the midst of the challenges before me. The passivity grew into a pattern of procrastination. I would wait to study and prepare for exams and projects hoping that I was smart enough to get it done on time and my grades not suffer.

Here's something to consider about the connection between passivity and procrastination: These two are cousins. They will always work well together. Graham Cooke said "Passivity and procrastination are habits of the flesh. We are dabbling at life rather than being engaged with it. Successful people do not drift to the top. It takes focus, discipline, and energy – all of which the Lord Jesus has in abundance!" **Procrastination is a destiny killer.** But God is a Way Maker. He is going to provide a way for you to kill procrastination in your life. You have to say "Yes" to His process.

During the college years, I was trying to will myself to overcome and not yield to Holy Spirit to help me overcome. In Christ, there is an abundance of everything that we need to overcome obstacles and challenges in our life. I've learned that we have to submit to the process of admitting, accepting, repenting, and yielding. This wouldn't develop for me until later in life. The procrastination and passivity took me down a path of mediocre performance. **Passivity and procrastination combined is a recipe for untapped potential.** I could have achieved more but these two cousins had a grip on me. There was the capacity to achieve at a higher level but I didn't lend myself to the discipline and sacrifice needed to go to the next level. You have a next level inside of you that God wants you to experience. You have to come to the place in your life where "enough is enough."

I had an "enough is enough" moment where the passivity in me died in the moment. Imagine having a "Christian" friend that knows how to preach, does well with others, and then you see the side of that friend that others don't get to see. Before I tell you the rest, I want you to keep this in mind.

Passivity dies in the presence of things you won't tolerate in your life. Maybe, right now, you're thinking of something that you've tolerated in your life for too long. If you continue to tolerate it long enough, it will begin to eat at you from the inside out. There are moments in your life that have caused you to fear failure, fear success, and fear moving forward. Now is an opportunity to be proactive and deal with the issue so that you can walk into the unknown. You can have peace in knowing that God is in your unknown.

This friend of mine took me into the unknown because I was about to respond to his behavior that I refused to tolerate. I was about to deal with a conflict in a way that I have never experienced before. I had a front row seat to his verbal abuse towards his girlfriend. It was a very coward move on his behalf to say the least. His actions pushed me over my red line. After she left, I did everything I could to cuss like a sailor. I let him have it! You would think that we were about to go fist-for-fist. Yet, it ended with us leaving each other's presence. Was it the best way for me to handle this? Did he deserve my response for his actions? My approach wasn't a Christian solution. Even in my immature attempt to solve the problem, he came to me and apologized for his actions. **Just because you get the right result, doesn't mean that your methods are pleasing to God.**

Please don't go out and tell people that Jefferson said it's okay to cuss people out when they do wrong. Hopefully you are beginning to think about that "thing" in your life that you've tolerated for too long. Overtime, if you allow certain actions and behaviors to continue in your life and/or the lives of others, these things will begin to impact others that are tied to the destiny and vision of your life. At this point there may be some of you waiting to hear what happened after I got slammed on the ground. Don't' worry. It's coming. Fast-forwarding to now, I can pull up a few situations where the passivity and procrastination in my life brought me to a new realization. I'm known for being gracious and very patient. Yet, God began to help me see how patience was a mask for my passivity and avoidance of conflict. **Don't allow a destiny-hindering character trait disguise itself as a high-quality character trait in your life.**

As a leader over the past few years, I let some things slide in ministry that I could have handled immediately. There was the fear of dealing with conflict because there was the fear of disagreement, fear of abandonment, and the fear of the unknown. I was passive when I should have been proactive. My passivity turned into procrastination, which led to people in the ministry being negatively affected. Instead of being proactive, I was being internally reactive and writing it off as being gracious and patient. I want you to pay attention here. **Internal reaction will lead to internal destruction.** As this began to happen, I came back to the place of "enough is enough". When this happened, I began to realize that my internal battle with passivity and procrastination resulted in an external impact in the lives of those that I loved. You may say that your struggle is only impacting you. The reality is that others will suffer from things that you don't address in your life. I reached that place of no longer tolerating certain behaviors that would not only cross boundaries in my life, but would also cross the boundaries in the lives of others.

The beauty in all of this is that even through my journey of going from passive to proactive, God has still allowed things to work out for my good. That means that the good and the bad that I have experienced isn't all working together for His glory to shine in my life. This brings me back to getting slammed on the ground. When I went up in the air, I didn't know what was going to happen. Even in the midst of the concrete, there was a softer place for me to hit the ground. Even in his anger, the mini-Goliath slammed me in the mulch. You're going to go through this process and it's going to be hard and you're going to hit the ground sometimes. Just know that you're going to be able to get up. It will hurt a little bit as you go through the process of learning how to be proactive. God's not going to allow you to be destroyed.

I've come to a season of my life where I'm going back to my college mentality of dealing with issues, head on, without the sailor mentality. I've made the choice to give **no more passes** to people and things that come to destroy the vision and assignment on my life. I'm giving no more passes for behaviors in my own life that would sabotage God's destiny on my life. There is too much in you to allow passivity and procrastination to kill the destiny that's inside of you. Consider this as you begin to make forward steps:

1. Identify issues in your life that you have been passive about. What things cause you to procrastinate and why?
2. Who can you talk to that will hold you accountable about being proactive?
3. Passive people tend to have no boundaries with people. You don't have to be

apologetic about setting boundaries and standing up for yourself and what's right.

4. Assertive doesn't mean you have to be aggressive.

5. Confrontation doesn't have to be negative. Confrontation is a healthy part of life that helps others know where you stand and what you will and will not tolerate.

6. Choose today to be proactive in your life. Fear can be present and you need to know that God is with you and will give you the courage to move forward.

Dedicated to my beautiful wife, Rosa, and my two sons, Peter and Abraham. Thank you for your love during the ups and downs of my life.

Jefferson J. Jones

Jefferson J. Jones (BS, Virginia Union University; M.Div., Liberty University) is the founder and pastor of Surge Ministries in Christiansburg, VA. He is a leader that is passionate about equipping and bringing healing into the lives of young adults to find their God-given identity. He also speaks at conferences and camps to encourage and inspire young people to live a Christ-centered life. He is one of the leaders of H.I.S., a ministry designed to bring positive change in the lives of men. Jefferson has been married to Rosa Carter Jones for 19 years. They have two young sons, Peter James and Abraham Joshua.

44

Support Jefferson J. Jones

Email: surgejjj@gmail.com

Facebook: https://www.facebook.com/JTriple

https://www.facebook.com/surgenrv

Instagram: @pastorjjj

Twitter: revjjjones529

Ecclesiastes 9:11

I returned, and saw under the sun, that the race is not to the swift, nor the battle to the strong, neither yet bread to the wise, nor yet riches to men of understanding, nor yet favour to men of skill; but time and chance happeneth to them all.

It was God's Turn
Dominic D. Davis

On December 12, 2017, my life completely changed! The day started off normal with morning coffee after prayer as I blasted music on the way to work. As the work day came to an end, I received a call saying, "You need to get to the rehab and see momma!" I replied; "I'm on my way." As soon as I ended the call, I received a text message saying. "Momma asked for you to come up here to the rehab to see her." Again, I replied, "I'm on way." My grandmother, who was the only mother I have ever known, had been dealing with congestive heart failure for months, but was in the rehab getting her strength back. When I arrived at the rehab, I was informed that she would not eat or drink. I told my family and the nursing staff that I will get her to eat and drink. Once the room was clear, Momma and I started talking as I proceeded to feed her. She didn't seem to have a problem eating for me.

Once she finished eating, I tucked her in and told her I would return in one hour after picking up my son from school. She replied, "I love you, but I will not be here when you get back." She has said this many times before, so I innocently replied, "Yes you will!" I gave her a kiss and told her I would return as soon as possible. She repeated, "I love you, baby, but I won't be here when you get back." I smiled and repeated, "Yes you will. I'll be back in one hour." As I was leaving, I turned back and she was smiling at me with this knowing look in her eye.

Forty minutes later, I was on my way back to the rehab and my phone rings. The voice on the other end yells, "GET TO THE REHAB, NOW! MOMMA IS UNRESPONSIVE!" My heart dropped and I broke the speed limit getting back to the rehab. As I walked into the entrance of the facility, I was told that Momma was gone! I could hear the blood pounding in my ears as I raced down the hallway as fast as I could. When I got to her room, time seemed to stop as I stared at my Momma's lifeless shell of the body in her chair. The air left my lungs and my heart dropped! It felt as though life began to leave me as I held on to her now cold hand. Although she had said it before, this time she knew that she wouldn't be alive when I returned. God had already told her and she was trying to tell me. My painful question was; "God, why didn't you tell me?

From that moment, I lost myself, my motivation, my faith, my focus, and my care for life was all gone. I didn't want to hear everything how everything was going to be okay. I didn't want to hear she was in a better place. I got upset every time someone said, "I'm praying for you!" Isolation became home for me. I shut everybody off and shut everything down. Depression became my normal, anger became a part of life, and tears became my sustenance. Everything was different now. My world had split open and nothing made sense. This is not how I thought it would be. Time had stopped. Nothing felt real. My mind could not stop replaying the events; hoping for a different outcome. The ordinary, everyday life, that others continued to inhabit, felt coarse and cruel. My appetite was nonexistent and I would stay up for two or three days at time.

Every object in my life became abstract and distorted; a shadow of the life that used to be. There was no place that this loss had not touched. I heard all manner of things: "She wouldn't want you to be sad. Everything happens for a reason. At least you had her as long as you did. You're strong, smart and resourceful, you will get through this and the experience will make you stronger." All of these sayings and seemingly kind gestures solved nothing. In fact, this kind of support only made me feel like no one in the world understood. This wasn't a paper cut or a fall off of a bike; this was goodbye to my mother. Days after her home-going service, I began to mentally drift into the darkest spots of life ever and struggled with deep depression. I finally decide to go see my doctor and was prescribed an anti-depressant and something to help with my sleep deprivation. Neither one helped.

A few days after New Year's Day, I remember driving around going absolutely nowhere and having this strong urge for alcohol. Up until this point, I had never tasted an alcoholic drink, but now the desire as overwhelming! I fought off the urge the first few nights, but then the urge got stronger and stronger. I began to search online for different drinks that could take the "edge off" and hopefully make me sleep or relax. I battled for months with these urges but never gave in, until the day of my birthday. I had cried all night and all day until I couldn't cry anymore. Depression had won. I grabbed my wallet, hopped in my car, and drove to the nearest bar. I had already decided that I was going to knock back about 3 or 4 drinks or as many as it would take to make the pain stop. If that didn't work, then I would continue to drink until I got kicked out! When I reached my destination, I got out and reached for my wallet, only to discover it wasn't there! in spite of the headache, the tears and stress, I know that I grabbed my wallet! Now, I'm on my knees in the car, searching for my wallet and it was nowhere to be found.

Angrily, I jumped back into the car and sped back home. I got out, ran upstairs to my room to look for my wallet, but it was not there. I went back downstairs to my car, lifted up the center console and there was my wallet! I started the car and drove back to the bar. Now the intensity was even higher and my mind was made up about drinking myself numb. By the time I got back to the bar, the place was surrounded with police and bar was shut down for business. Now, I was even more upset as I drove to the nearest store and went straight to the liquor section. I grabbed four, big bottles of liquor and proceeded to the register. As I'm standing in line, I look up and the man in front of me has on a shirt that says *"God is our refuge and strength, always ready to help in times of trouble"* (Psalm 46:1, The Living Bible translation).

Right then and there I said' "GOD, I NEED YOU! I'M IN TROUBLE AND CAN'T TAKE THIS PAIN ANYMORE! PLEASE, HELP ME! I'LL GET OUT OF THE WAY! JUST HELP ME!" The people in the store just stood there; looking at me. I walked out, crying and I could feel God wrap His arms around me. When I got back into my car, I said, "God, you have to help. I've been trying to hold on. Trying to keep going, but I can't anymore. Lord I'm hurting. I'm weak. I'm broken and alone. I've been trying to do this on my own, but I just can't. God it's on you!" I sat in the corner of my office, at home, all night and I could still feel the same arms wrapped around me, hugging me tight! No one was in the room with me, but God was there! For the first time in months, I stopped crying, got in the bed and went to sleep.

I had slept for an entire day and I woke up to "Be Still" by Travis Green, playing on the TV. I could hear God saying, "Son, be still and know that I Am God. I got you." At that point It was HIS TURN! God ended that deep level of depression and killed the desire for alcohol that was setup to kill me. As the weeks rolled by, God began to restore my mental stability and strength. I still cried, but it was no longer a cry of devastation. If I would not have stopped trying to do it my way and kept fighting my own fight, I would've lost my life. BUT, THANKS BE UNTO GOD for being my refuge, my strength, and THAT very present help in the time of trouble. I know without a doubt that God saved my life for such a time as this! However, it started when I acknowledged that it was His turn!

Dedicated to my grandmother (Momma), the late Evangelist Lucille Davis. Your unfailing love and prayers for me was without pause. I thank God for you daily and appreciate the life that you lived and the life that you birthed in me. You told me to "stay with Jesus" and that is exactly what I will continue to do. Rest in Heaven, Mom. Thank you! Love you!

Dominic D. Davis

Dominic D. Davis is a genuine, loving, family man who resides in Indianapolis, Indiana, where he was born and raised. Dominic is an ordained minister of the Pentecostal Assemblies of the World (P.A.W.). His love for the Lord can be seen in how he cares for his natural and spiritual family. In 2016, Dominic founded the international brand, "bragonGod", which has been displayed throughout the United States, Europe, Africa and London.

Support Dominic D. Davis

Email: mrddavis8@gmail.com

Facebook: www.facebook.com/ComebackDavis

Instagram: @mr.d.davis, @bragonGod

When Enough Is Enough
Kanshasa T. Downs

On the night of March 7th 2017, I spent my evening at a military police station. I was not there because I was being arrested or because I was reporting for duty. I was there because I was a victim of domestic abuse. I was not physically harmed because I ran from the scene and evaded all hazards. I mean, I LITERALLY ran. My wife, at the time, tried to run me over with a truck and had authorities also confiscated large kitchen knives from the vehicle. Nothing I did was able to defuse the situation. The scene was not calm until the military police had her in cuffs and in for questioning. This scene was my first encounter of that kind and magnitude. There are times in life we will come face-to-face with something that will change us for life. We are the ones that have to decide how it is going to change us. Is it going to be something that is going hinder us or propel us? "Enough is enough" is a phrase that when we get tired of being hindered, we set our minds to stand on top of what was hindering us and we use it to propel us. I have come to realize that we have a designed purpose and nothing should stop us from getting to that purpose, not even our own lack of knowledge, laziness or outside opposition. There have been several times in my life I where I had to meet my own deficiencies, eye to eye. There were also moments when my opposition was a precedent set by generations before me. Finally, there were external opponents that caused me harm.

Now back to my most extreme encounter, which in this case deals with relationships. My dealing with relationships is truly a combination of precedents set before and external opponents. I had seen some abuse as a child, so my goal was to never be around it as an adult. But in many of my relationships with certain individuals, this was normal and I was not capable of identifying the red flags in potential mates before it got too far. The second marriage ended with the scene in the introduction with my life and career on the line at the military police station. That was the breaking point, but let us start at the beginning.

As we started the courtship, things seemed normal but the signs were there. I had mistaken control for passion and concern. I was isolated from my family and told not talk to any female friends from the start. She was offended by me talking to any female in any capacity, especially someone from my past. I have four children from my first marriage and she was offended by any conversation I had with them or their mother. So I would leave the room whenever I had phone conversations with anyone. Not because I was doing something shady, but because of how she felt. Infidelity was never in my vocabulary, so I was not worried about. However, because she had been cheated on in the past and it became one of her greatest fears. I was naïve and would let her listen in on a few conversations, without the other party's knowledge, to show her that everything was on the up and up. Because I did not have bad blood or hate when I spoke to my former spouse, she was offended by that. There was one incident in which I should have drawn the line and made a quick exit, as fast as possible, out of the relationship.

I was stationed in North Carolina and she was my girlfriend, at the time. Out of the blue, she got offended about some messenger chats. One messenger chat showed me talking to a longtime friend about construction and yard work. I sent a video of how to build a small pond in the back yard because she has her own construction business. My girlfriend believed that I deleted messages and that I was talking code while being inappropriate. This became commonplace for her to read her own story into any conversation I had with anyone. The second message entailed me talking to someone taking a class I had just finished and there was nothing wrong or out of line. Now, looking back at the situation, I should have distanced myself at that time. But I told myself, "She is not use to a good man and things would get better." I was so wrong! There were other similar scenes like that, but those were early enough to end the madness before it started.

Another red flag, that should have made me stop in my tracks, was the names she used to call herself. This should standout to anyone! The Bible says, "Love your neighbor as yourself," but she could not even love herself. She even took back the original ring that I chose and got one ten times cheaper. Was it her being money savvy or her not felling she was worth ring? There has to be something wrong with the devaluing of oneself to that degree. As I fast forward, we began to make plans for the future and had a quick wedding with my sister and her husband. With a larger wedding planned for later, I was in beyond where I had been before. However, things did not get better.

Things were calm for a brief moment as I went to work and she stayed home. She was being lied to by others in her own ministry circles, but the biggest issue was what was going on in her mind. and her own mind was the bigger case. She had children from a previous relationship and would use her fifteen year old to check up on me, which should have been another sign that something was not quite right. She traveled for speaking engagements and when I was home relaxing with the kids, she would call and or message her son to monitor my movements as if I was under surveillance. There was nothing to report because there was nothing going on. The accusation became more frequent and more outrageous as time went on. Now, I understand this was her reliving events from her past relationships. I was not the arguing type, but if we had a disagreement, she would want to argue all night just because. When I did not respond to her arguing, she got abusive and hit me. This was major because I had never been in a relationship that involved any type of violence. Not only was this not me, but domestic violence is a military career ender. This was one of the things from my childhood that I was not to get entangled with.

There was a season of me enabling her, but she would admit that she was wrong and stated she was going to get better. Since you are reading this, we know that did not happen. The honeymoon season of abuse did not last long, but that day on March 7th, would be the final straw. That day started off calm. She stated that it was ok for us to be over and she said she would give me a divorce. We talked that morning and I went to work and was going to do the paperwork. I came home later that day with the papers and placed them in her hand. The kids needed picked up from school, so I changed clothes and preceded to pick them up. Unlike before, she decided she wanted to ride with me. After we returned, the kids went inside, while she and I talked. As we talked, she asked to see my phone. I said, "NO!" and rage came over her as she climbed over the seat to get my phone that had I placed it in the door of the SUV. I told her there was no point in carrying on, she has the divorce papers.

Let me take a step back. We tried several different counseling sessions; from professional on the base to the Chaplain. I even had my own counselor and throughout all of this, I remember one of the sessions and my therapist saying, "When are you going to get off the roller coaster?" Enough was enough and it was time to get off that roller coaster now! So as she climbed over the seat, she began to call me names. I left the house and she followed me a few blocks down the street. I called my command and told them what was happening. After that, I got on the phone with my sister and she recorded some of the adventure.

I went down the street and different places as she was looking for me in the SUV. I could literally hear the music from the movie "Friday" playing in my head. The music every time D-bow showed up. She found me in the gym and took my phones. At this point, I did not care! I was just trying to get away. She saw me outside and tried to run me over! She stopped the vehicle pulled out kitchen knives, and screamed, "I'M GOING TO KILL YOU FOR RUINING MY LIFE!" She called people with my phone, including one of my sisters. I felt like I was in my own Tyler Perry movie. Someone saw that I was in distress and immediately called the military police. They, along with NCIS, interviewed me and conducted an investigation, but there was nothing much they could do because she was not in the military. They informed me that they would have to turn her over to the civilian police. All of a sudden, she managed to faint and was taken to the hospital. That night, I ended up staying at a base facility, while she was taken in for questioning. March 7, 2017 was my enough point! It took several months to get there, but that is what it took for me. That day, that moment when I finally decided to say, "NO!" was enough!

Later that month, I filed for divorce because I was no longer waiting on her to agree to anything. From the date of marriage to the time I filed for divorce, we had only been married only eight months. She dragged out the divorce proceedings, but a little over a year later, it was finally over! To think that day started with a simple agreement and me giving her the choice of how she wanted to end this dysfunctional and abusive relationship. I was strong enough to put up with it that long. Just because you are strong enough to handle situations, does not mean that you should have to. I made it and anyone reading this can to. I pray no one would have to go through any of what I went through, but there are times and situations that are presented in our lives that will push us to make a change. God has to make us uncomfortable or we would never move. It's in those times that we have to know when we have had enough and allow Him to have His turn!

2 Corinthians 4:8-11

We are troubled on every side, yet not distressed; we are perplexed, but not in despair; Persecuted, but not forsaken; cast down, but not destroyed; Always bearing about in the body the dying of the Lord Jesus, that the life also of Jesus might be made manifest in our body. For we which live are always delivered unto death for Jesus' sake, that the life also of Jesus might be made manifest in our mortal flesh

Kanshasa T. Downs

Kanshasa T. Downs was born in the small town of Sylvester, Georgia, but God had big plans for him. A determined student, he excelled in the classroom and on the track. Shortly after receiving his high school diploma, he earned the title of United States Marine. In more than 20 years of honorable service, he has been stationed both home and abroad. It was during this time that he became the father to his four daughters. God's calling upon his life grew and he answered by earning his ordination as well as graduate degrees in Divinity and Pastoral counseling, with focus on addictions and recovery, from Liberty University. In his spare time, he enjoys playing rugby, watching football, and spending time with his family. He currently resides in Southern California. Elder Downs looks forward to dedicating himself to fully helping others unlock the keys to the Kingdom of God.

Support Kanshasa T. Downs

Email: downskt@gmail.com

Facebook: www.facebook.com/Pastortyronedowns

Instagram: @the_tyrone_downs

Twitter: @ktdowns

Periscope: @ktdowns

About H.I.S.

Vision

To have men seek and claim their rightful place in society and their homes in order to be a vital and contributing member in their communities. To lead by example and inspire other men to do the same while providing unity to help men motivate one another to strive for greatness.

Mission

Our mission is to actively help men to realize and utilize their God-given ability to better themselves, their communities, and their families. To Heal, Inspire, and Support men of all ages, races, and nationalities through conferences, seminars, workshops, and mentorship programs.

Support H.I.S.

For more information on how you can support of become a part of the H.I.S. Men's Outreach Ministry, contact us at histurn2017@gmail.com.

Follow H.I.S.

Facebook: www.facebook.com/histurn2017

Instagram: @histurn2017

Twitter: @histurn2017